SET UP THE SKELETON

By Kirsty Holmes

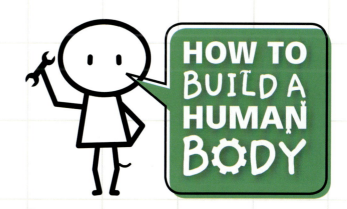

HOW TO BUILD A HUMAN BODY

Published in 2021 by Enslow Publishing, LLC
101 W. 23rd Street, Suite 240,
New York, NY 10011

Copyright © 2021 Booklife Publishing
This editon is published by arrangment with Booklife Publishing

All rights reserved.

No part of this book may be reproduced by any means without the written permission of the publisher.

Cataloging-in-Publication Data

Names: Holmes, Kirsty.
Title: Set up the skeleton / Kirsty Holmes.
Description: New York : Enslow Publishing, 2021. | Series: How to build a human body | Includes glossary and index.
Identifiers: ISBN 9781978519275 (pbk.) | ISBN 9781978519299 (library bound) | ISBN 9781978519282 (6 pack)
Subjects: LCSH: Human skeleton--Juvenile literature. | Bones--Juvenile literature.
Classification: LCC QP301.H65 2020 | DDC 612.7'5--dc23

Printed in the United States of America

CPSIA compliance information: Batch #BS20ENS: For further information contact Enslow Publishing, New York, New York at 1-800-542-2595

Photo credits:
Images are courtesy of Shutterstock.com.
With thanks to Getty Images, Thinkstock Photo and iStockphoto.

Ian Struction - gjee. Grid - DistanceO. Front Cover - Mr. Luck, Trish Volt. 4 - VAygun Aliyeva. 5 - brgfx. 6–7 - Olga Bolbot. 8 - Olga Bolbot. 9 - eranicle. 10 - Pretty Vectors, Maxim Cherednichenko. 11 - GzP_Design. 12 - MSSA. 13 - Pretty Vectors. 14 - EstherQueen999. 15 - EstherQueen999, ducu59us, eranicle. 17 - Timonina. 20 - Pensiri, KenshiDesign, Christos Georghiou, Fox Design. 21 - vvushakovv, davooda, Hein Nouwens, HN Works, davooda, Alexandr III, Farah Sadikhova, origami cat, Martial Red, Farhads. 22 - Alice July. 23 - FernPat, Victoria Sergeeva.

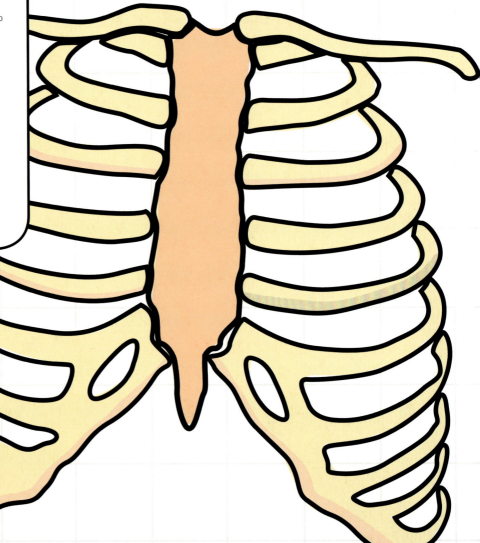

CONTENTS

Page 4	The Body Builders
Page 6	The Human Body
Page 8	The Human Skeleton
Page 10	Bits and Bones
Page 12	Put It All Together
Page 14	Marvelous Marrow
Page 16	Check It's Working
Page 18	Care for Your Skeleton: Exercise
Page 20	Care for Your Skeleton: Food
Page 22	Activities
Page 24	Glossary and Index

Words that look like this can be found in the glossary on page 24.

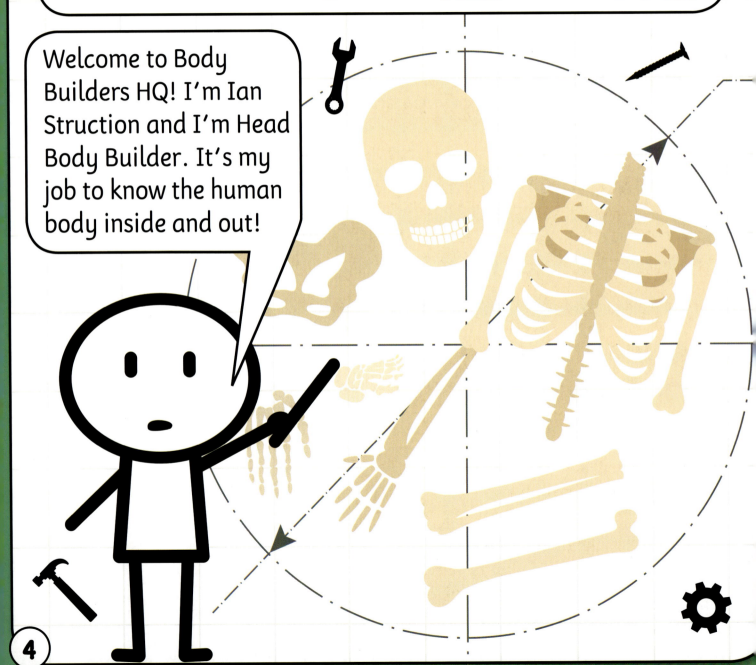

This instruction manual will teach you all about the human skeleton. Look out for these signs to help you understand:

Do this

Don't do this

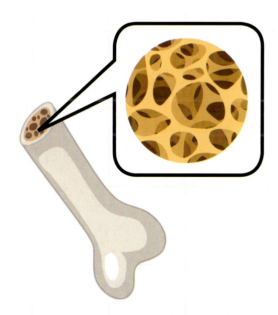

Zoom in on details

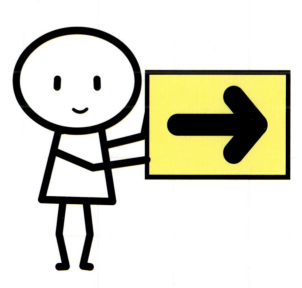

More information

THE HUMAN BODY

Your body is an incredible machine. It is very complicated and very clever. You have lots of <u>organs</u> in your body and each one has an important job to do.

blood and marrow

bones and joints

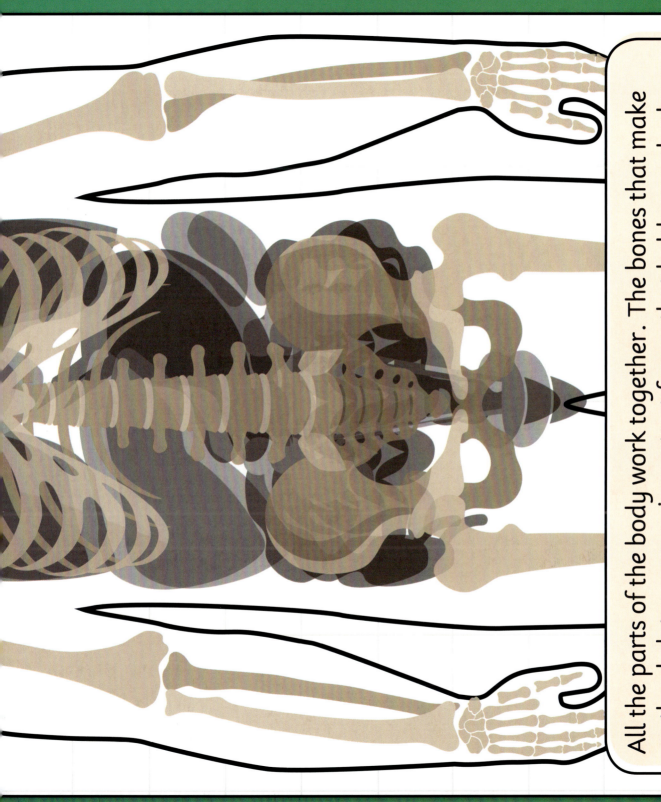

All the parts of the body work together. The bones that make up the skeleton are an important frame that holds your body up.

THE HUMAN SKELETON

The skeleton is made up of over 200 different bones. Your skeleton stops you from being a wobbly bag of skin on the floor!

- adults have 206 bones
- protects the soft organs inside
- grows as we grow
- lets us move around

The place where a bone is connected to another one is called a joint.

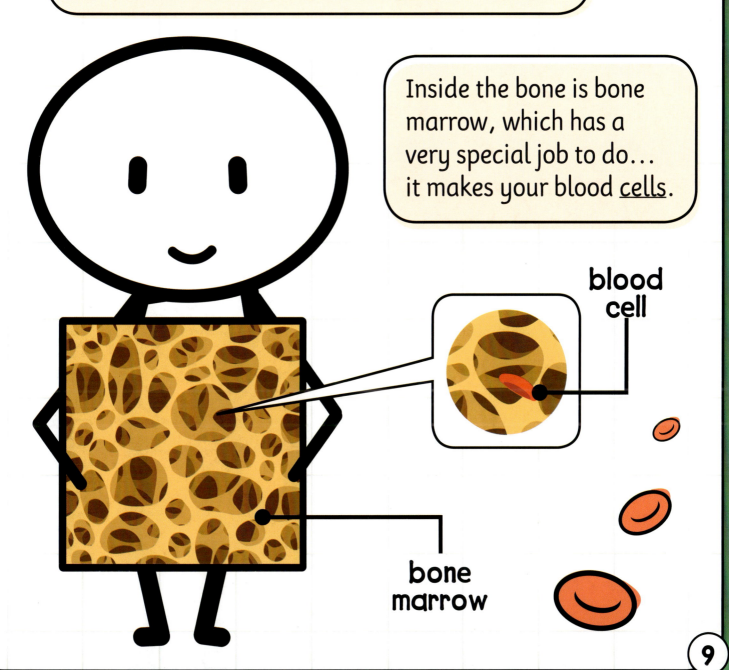

BITS AND BONES

For the Body Builders to set up this skeleton, we will need lots of parts. Here are the bones for an adult skeleton.

spine 24x vertebrae, 1x sacrum, 1x coccyx

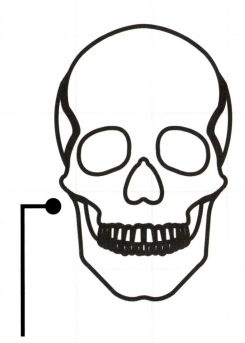

skull 29x bones

ribs 24x ribs, 1x sternum

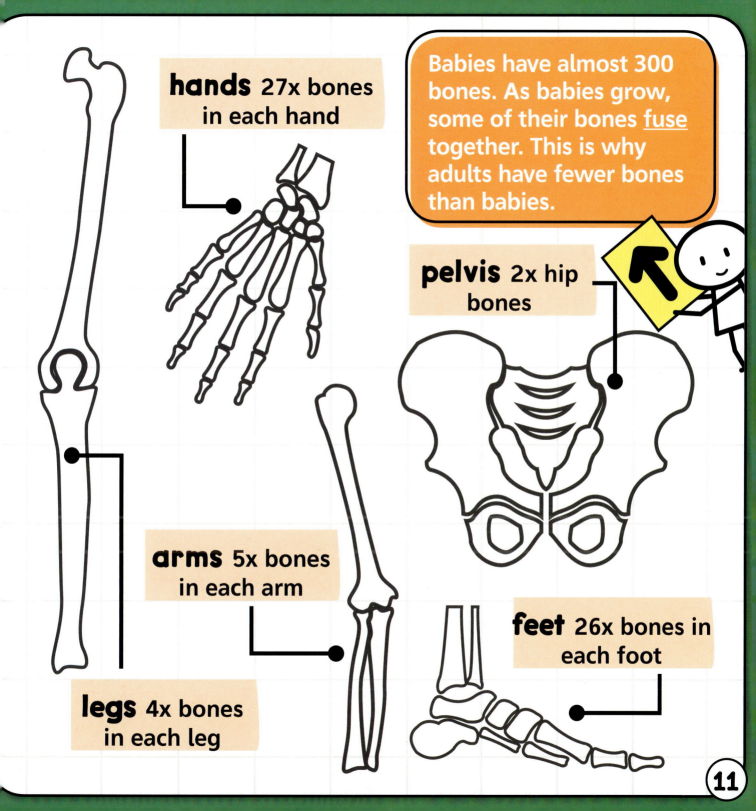

PUT IT ALL TOGETHER

The bones of the skeleton are held together by joints. Joints are made of soft tissue. This lets your bones move easily.

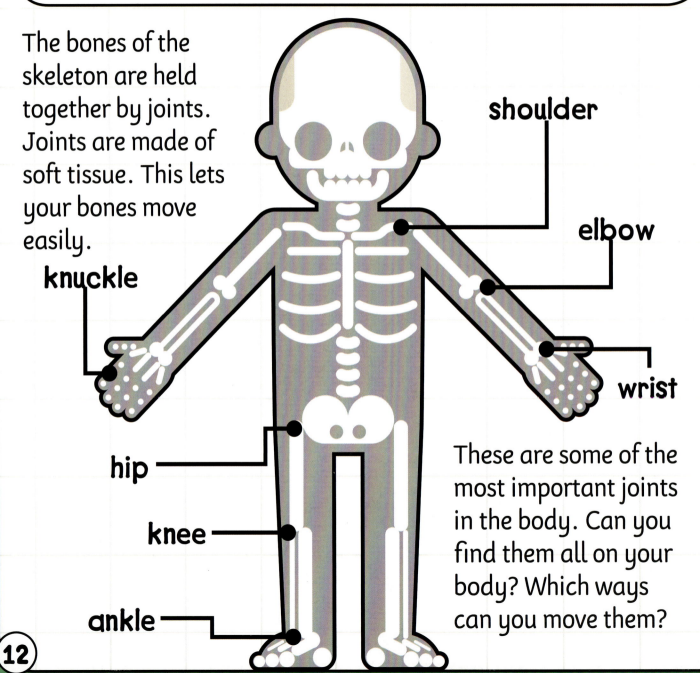

shoulder

elbow

knuckle

wrist

hip

knee

ankle

These are some of the most important joints in the body. Can you find them all on your body? Which ways can you move them?

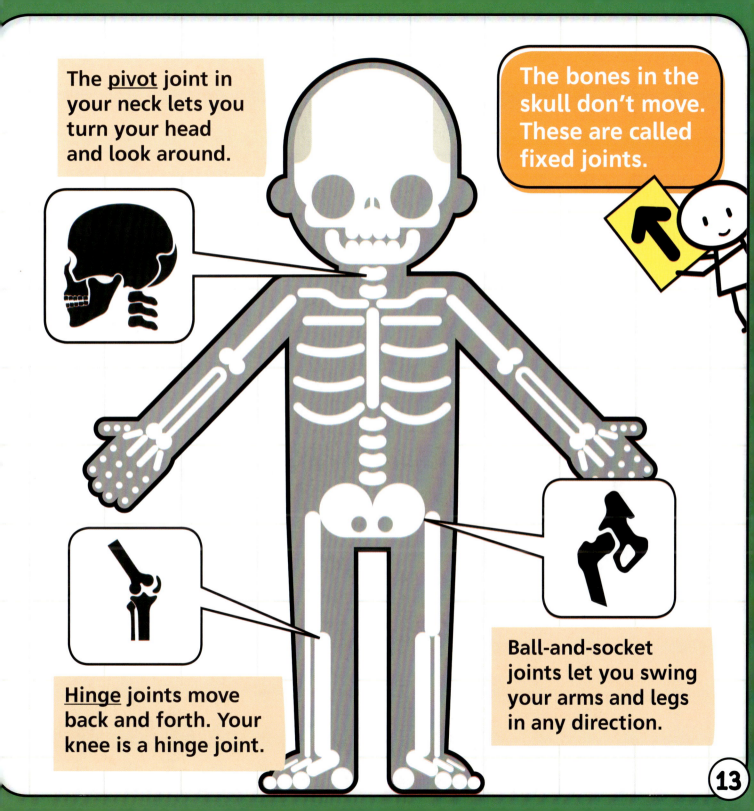

MARVELOUS MARROW

Inside many of our bones, there is a spongy tissue called bone marrow. There are two types of bone marrow: red and yellow.

Red marrow makes new blood cells, and is mostly in the shoulders, skull, and long, flat bones such as the thigh bone.

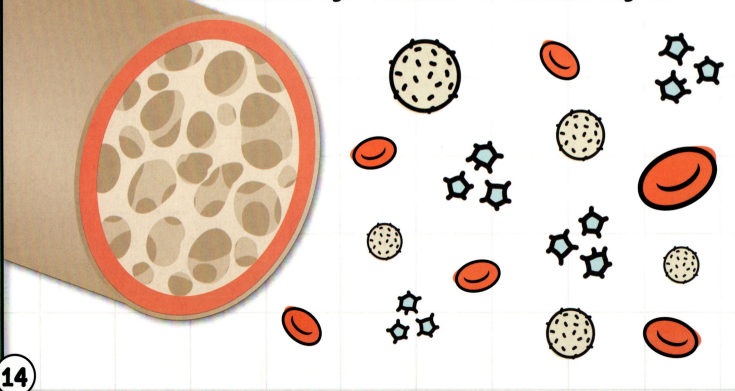

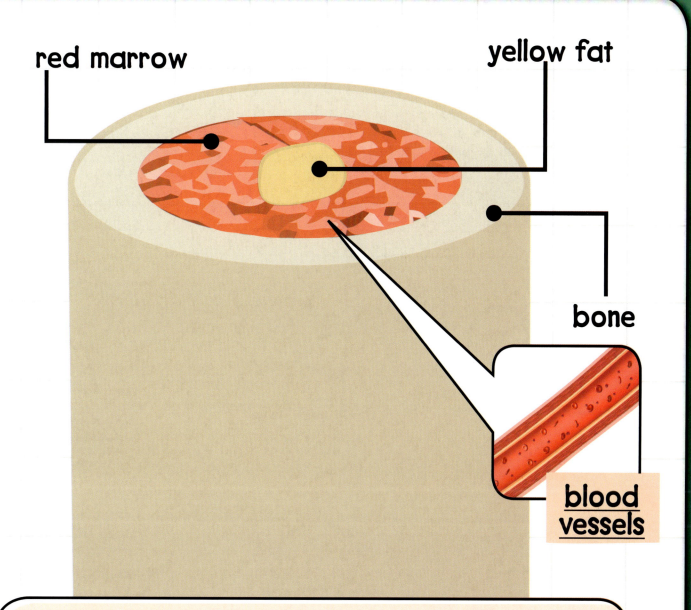

As you get older, your bone has more fat in it, which is why it looks yellow. Yellow bone marrow stores fat. In an emergency, it can make even more red blood cells.

CHECK IT'S WORKING

Try these yoga poses to see if your bones and joints are working well.

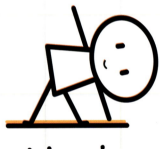
triangle

standing bow

tree

half moon

warrior

downward dog

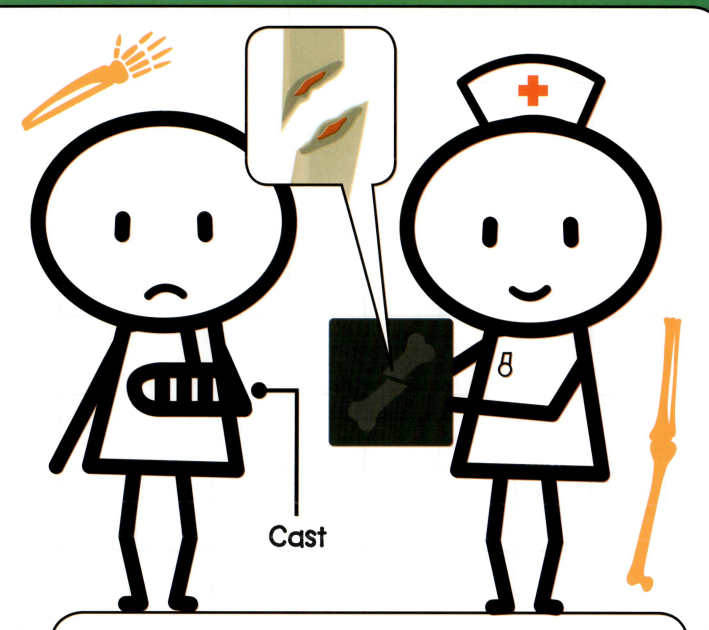

Cast

If we fall over awkwardly, our bones can break. Don't worry—bones fix themselves after a while. You might need a cast to make sure you heal correctly.

CARE FOR YOUR SKELETON: EXERCISE

Your bones do most of their growing while you are young. Make sure you get plenty of exercise while you are growing to make sure your bones grow strong and healthy.

gymnastics

skipping rope

dancing

jumping

Building healthy bones when you are young will help prevent bone problems when you are older.

running

trampoline

martial arts

hopscotch

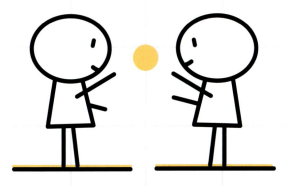

ball games

CARE FOR YOUR SKELETON: FOOD

Calcium-rich foods

Your bones need calcium to grow. Your body also needs vitamin D to be able to <u>absorb</u> calcium. Eating these foods together will make your bones stronger.

milk

sardines

soybeans

Food with calcium added

cereal

bread

soy milk

Vitamin D-rich foods

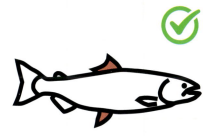
salmon

tuna

eggs

red meat

shrimp

vitamin supplement

Not bone-boosting foods

sugary food

salt

soda

ACTIVITIES

Protect Your Noggin

Get Some Sun

Always wear a helmet to protect your head when using your bike or scooter.

You can also get vitamin D from sunlight—so why not get outside to play, or have a calcium-rich snack at a picnic?

Skeleton Sandwich

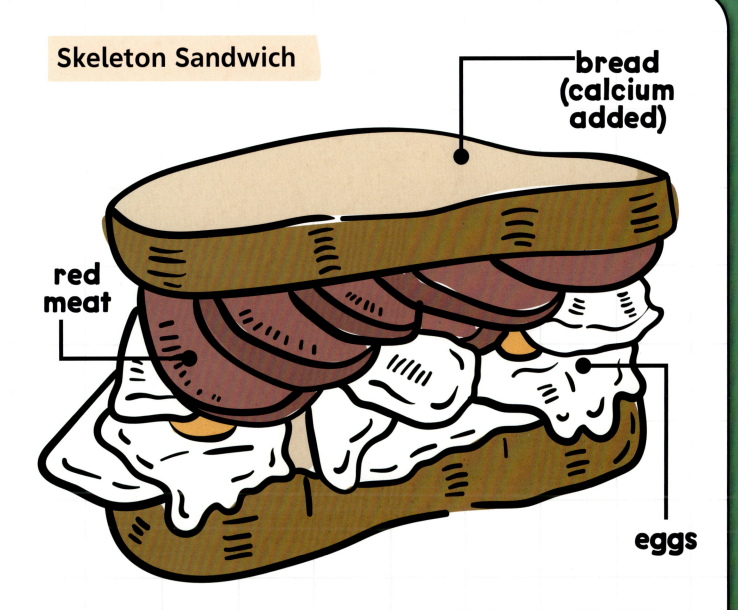

Can you imagine a sandwich that contains a calcium-rich food and a vitamin D-rich food? How many bone-boosting foods can you fit into one sandwich? Now draw it!

GLOSSARY

absorb to take in or soak up

blood vessels tubes in the body that blood moves through

cast a hard shell used to protect a broken bone

cells the basic units that make up all living things

fuse to join together

hinge a type of joint that opens and closes

organs parts of the body that have specific jobs to do

pivot to move or swing back and forth

supplement a pill taken to make someone healthier

tissue a group of cells in the body that, together, do a similar job

INDEX

bones 6–21

breaks 17

growth 8, 11, 18, 20

hinge 13

joints 6, 8, 12–13, 16

marrow 6, 9, 14–15

organs 6, 8

pivot 13

tissue 9, 12, 14